Love Rekindled

Love Rekindled

Matthew Petchinsky

Love Rekindled: Reigniting Passion in Relationships
By: Matthew Petchinsky

Introduction

Strategies for Strengthening Love: A Foundation for Rekindling Passion

Love is one of the most profound and transformative emotions humans experience. It is the cornerstone of our relationships, the bedrock of our happiness, and a source of resilience during life's most challenging times. Yet, even the strongest relationships can face moments of strain, stagnation, or disconnection. The beautiful reality is that love is not a finite resource—it evolves, adapts, and can be rekindled when both partners commit to nurturing it.

This book, *Love Rekindled: Reigniting Passion in Relationships*, is a roadmap for couples seeking to breathe new life into their partnership. Whether you are confronting obstacles such as miscommunication, emotional distance, or the demands of a busy life, the strategies outlined here are designed to rebuild emotional intimacy, deepen mutual understanding, and reignite the spark that initially brought you together.

The Nature of Love and Connection

Love is not static; it is a living, dynamic bond that thrives on attention, care, and effort. Like a garden, it requires nurturing to flourish. Over time, relationships may falter not due to a lack of love but due to unspoken frustrations, unmet expectations, or life's relentless pace overshadowing moments of connection. Understanding this truth is the first step toward transformation: love can always be renewed and strengthened with intentionality.

Why Rekindling Passion Matters

Passion is often the most vivid expression of love. It's the spark that fuels attraction, creates intimacy, and fosters a sense of belonging. Yet passion often wanes over time—not because the love is gone but because it becomes buried beneath routine, stress, and familiarity. Rekindling passion is not just about restoring physical intimacy; it's about rediscovering your partner in new ways, creating shared experiences, and celebrating the uniqueness of your bond.

Overcoming Common Barriers

Rebuilding love and passion in a relationship requires identifying and overcoming common barriers. These may include:

1. **Communication Breakdowns** – Unspoken feelings, assumptions, or unresolved conflicts can erode the foundation of trust and connection.
2. **Emotional Distance** – Over time, couples may drift apart, feeling more like roommates than romantic partners.
3. **The Pressures of Daily Life** – Work demands, financial stress, and parenting responsibilities can leave little time for nurturing a relationship.
4. **Unrealistic Expectations** – The idealized version of love portrayed in media often leads to disappointment when real relationships face challenges.

Through proven strategies and thoughtful practices, this book addresses these barriers head-on, offering actionable steps to overcome them and foster a deeper, more fulfilling connection.

What You'll Find in This Book

In the chapters that follow, we'll explore a wide range of tools, techniques, and philosophies to help you strengthen your bond and reignite passion:

- **Rebuilding Emotional Intimacy** – Learn how to open up, listen deeply, and create a safe space for vulnerability.
- **Reigniting Physical Connection** – Discover ways to prioritize intimacy and rekindle desire through meaningful gestures, thoughtful surprises, and shared experiences.
- **Cultivating Mindfulness in Love** – Develop habits that keep you present, attentive, and appreciative of your partner's unique qualities.
- **Communication Strategies** – Master the art of speaking and listening with intention to resolve conflicts and build trust.
- **Creating Shared Joy** – Explore ways to infuse fun, laughter, and spontaneity into your relationship.
- **Healing and Forgiveness** – Address past hurts and create a pathway toward understanding, acceptance, and renewed commitment.

Each chapter includes practical exercises, reflective questions, and inspiring real-life stories to help you tailor these strategies to your relationship. Whether you are newly married, in a long-term partnership, or navigating a period of transition, these tools are designed to empower you to cultivate lasting love.

The Journey Begins

Strengthening love is not about perfection—it's about growth, resilience, and embracing the imperfections that make your relationship uniquely yours. It requires patience, compassion, and an open heart. As you embark on this journey, remember that even the smallest steps can yield transformative results.

Love Rekindled is more than a guide—it's an invitation to rediscover the joy, passion, and connection that first drew you together. With intention, effort, and mutual commitment, the love you share can become even stronger than before.

Chapter 1: Reflecting on Your Journey Together

Every relationship has a story—a journey filled with moments of joy, trials, growth, and transformation. The act of reflecting on this journey is a powerful first step in reigniting the love and passion within your relationship. By looking back, you gain clarity about where you began, how far you've come, and the areas that need attention and care.

This chapter invites you and your partner to explore your shared history, celebrate your milestones, and examine the challenges that have shaped your bond. Reflection is not just an exercise in nostalgia; it is a pathway to understanding, gratitude, and intentional growth.

The Importance of Reflection in Relationships

Reflection allows couples to reconnect with their shared narrative. It's easy to lose sight of your journey when daily routines, responsibilities, and stressors dominate your attention. Revisiting the key moments in your relationship helps rekindle a sense of gratitude, foster mutual understanding, and identify areas that may need healing or improvement.

Reflection serves several purposes:

1. **Fosters Gratitude:** Revisiting happy memories reminds you of the joy and love that brought you together.
2. **Builds Empathy:** Understanding your partner's perspective during pivotal moments can deepen your emotional bond.
3. **Identifies Growth Areas:** Reflecting on challenges reveals patterns, behaviors, or unresolved issues that need attention.
4. **Inspires Renewal:** Celebrating your shared history creates a foundation for building an even stronger future.

Guided Reflection: Where It All Began

Take a moment to revisit the origins of your relationship. Ask yourselves:

- How did you meet, and what were your first impressions of each other?
- What initially attracted you to your partner?
- What memories stand out from your early days together?

These questions remind you of the excitement and passion that sparked your relationship. Reflecting on these moments can bring a sense of nostalgia and help you reconnect with the love that drew you together in the first place.

Celebrating Milestones

Relationships are built on shared experiences—both big and small. Identify and celebrate your milestones:

- **Firsts:** Your first date, first vacation, or the first time you said, "I love you."
- **Achievements:** Milestones like buying a home, starting a family, or overcoming a major challenge together.
- **Everyday Joys:** Quiet moments that define your connection, like cooking together, laughing over an inside joke, or supporting each other through tough days.

As you reflect on these moments, express gratitude for the ways they've strengthened your bond. Share with your partner how these experiences made you feel and why they are meaningful.

Exploring Challenges and Growth

Every relationship faces challenges, and these moments often define the strength and resilience of a partnership. Reflect on the obstacles you've faced together:

- What challenges tested your relationship, and how did you navigate them?
- What did you learn about yourself and your partner during those times?
- Are there unresolved issues that still linger?

Approaching this reflection with honesty and compassion is crucial. Rather than assigning blame, focus on what these experiences taught you and how they contributed to your growth as individuals and as a couple.

Creating a Relationship Timeline

One practical exercise for reflection is creating a relationship timeline. On a piece of paper or using a digital tool, map out the key moments in your journey together. Include:

- Positive milestones (e.g., your wedding day, moving in together).
- Challenges (e.g., a significant argument, periods of distance).
- Transformative moments (e.g., making a major decision, supporting each other through a difficult time).

Reviewing this timeline together can help you see your relationship as a dynamic, evolving story. It also offers insight into the patterns, behaviors, and events that have shaped your bond.

A Gratitude Ritual for Reflection

Gratitude is a cornerstone of a strong relationship. Set aside time to share what you appreciate about each other. Use the following prompts:

- "I'm grateful for the way you..."
- "One thing you've done that has meant a lot to me is..."
- "I admire you for..."

Expressing gratitude helps shift focus from frustrations to the positive aspects of your relationship. It also reminds both partners of the qualities and actions that make your connection special.

The Role of Reflection in Moving Forward

Reflection is not about dwelling on the past—it's about learning from it. As you examine your journey, ask yourselves:

- What moments or patterns do we want to recreate in our future?
- What lessons from our challenges can we apply to strengthen our bond?
- How can we celebrate our growth while continuing to evolve as a couple?

This process of looking back with intention paves the way for deeper understanding and mutual commitment.

Exercises for Deeper Reflection

1. **The Memory Jar:** Write down individual memories that brought you joy, laughter, or love. Place them in a jar and take turns reading them aloud. This activity helps you relive positive experiences and reinforces your connection.
2. **Letter to Your Past Selves:** Write letters to your younger selves at the start of your relationship. Share what you've learned and what you wish you had known. Exchange letters and discuss how these lessons have shaped your relationship.
3. **Revisit Special Places:** Spend time in a location that holds significance for your relationship, such as where you first met or had your first date. Reflect on how far you've come since then.

Conclusion: Honoring Your Story

Reflecting on your journey together is a deeply personal and transformative act. It allows you to honor your shared history, appreciate the growth you've achieved, and set the stage for a renewed and thriving connection. Remember, every relationship is a story in progress, and by acknowledging your past, you equip yourselves to write the next chapter with intention, passion, and love.

As you move forward in this book, let the insights from your reflection serve as a foundation for the strategies, tools, and practices that will help you reignite the spark and deepen your bond. Your journey is unique, and the love you've shared is worth celebrating—and strengthening.

Chapter 2: Communicating with Love and Respect

Communication is the lifeblood of any relationship. It is the bridge that connects thoughts, emotions, and intentions between partners, fostering understanding, trust, and intimacy. However, communication can often be fraught with challenges, including misunderstandings, assumptions, or unspoken frustrations. When partners learn to communicate with love and respect, they create a foundation for deeper connection and resilience.

In this chapter, we explore the principles, strategies, and practices that enable couples to cultivate a loving and respectful dialogue. Whether you're navigating difficult conversations or seeking to enhance everyday interactions, mastering compassionate communication will empower you to strengthen your bond and rekindle your passion.

The Power of Communication in Relationships

Effective communication is more than just talking; it involves active listening, empathy, and the ability to express yourself authentically. When communication falters, even minor issues can escalate into significant conflicts. Conversely, when partners communicate with love and respect, they:

- Build mutual trust and understanding.
- Resolve conflicts constructively.
- Deepen emotional intimacy and connection.
- Foster a sense of safety and belonging.

Key Principles of Loving and Respectful Communication

1. **Prioritize Emotional Safety**
   A relationship thrives when both partners feel safe expressing their thoughts and emotions without fear of judgment, criticism, or rejection. Emotional safety involves:
   - Creating a nonjudgmental space for dialogue.
   - Validating each other's feelings, even when you disagree.
   - Avoiding blame, sarcasm, or dismissive comments.

2. **Practice Empathy**
   Empathy is the ability to understand and share your partner's feelings. It requires putting yourself in their shoes and viewing the situation from their perspective. Empathy can be practiced by:
   - Asking open-ended questions to explore your partner's emotions.
   - Acknowledging their feelings with statements like, "I understand why you feel that way."
   - Responding with compassion rather than defensiveness.

3. **Express Yourself Clearly and Honestly**
   Miscommunication often arises from vague or indirect expressions. Speak clearly and assertively, sharing your thoughts, needs, and emotions in a way that invites understanding rather than conflict. Use "I" statements to express your feelings without assigning blame, such as:
   - "I feel hurt when I'm not included in decisions because it makes me feel unimportant."

4. **Listen to Understand, Not to Respond**
   Listening is an active process that goes beyond hearing words. To listen with love and respect:
   - Maintain eye contact and avoid distractions.
   - Resist the urge to interrupt or offer solutions prematurely.

- Reflect on what your partner has said by paraphrasing or summarizing their points.

Breaking Down Barriers to Communication

1. **Overcoming Defensive Reactions**
   Defensive responses can derail a conversation and escalate tension. To manage defensiveness:
   - Take a moment to pause and breathe before responding.
   - Focus on the issue at hand rather than assigning blame.
   - Remind yourself that your partner's feedback is an opportunity for growth, not an attack.
2. **Addressing Emotional Triggers**
   Past experiences or unresolved issues can create emotional triggers that hinder communication. To navigate these triggers:
   - Identify patterns or situations that evoke strong reactions.
   - Share your triggers with your partner to build awareness and understanding.
   - Work together to develop strategies for managing these moments constructively.
3. **Avoiding Communication Pitfalls**
   Common pitfalls in communication include:
   - **Stonewalling:** Shutting down or withdrawing from the conversation.
   - **Criticism:** Attacking your partner's character rather than addressing specific behaviors.
   - **Contempt:** Expressing disdain through sarcasm, ridicule, or eye-rolling.
   - **Interrupting:** Cutting your partner off before they've finished speaking.
     Overcoming these pitfalls requires patience, self-awareness, and a commitment to respectful dialogue.

Practical Strategies for Effective Communication

1. **The 5:1 Ratio**
   Research shows that successful relationships maintain a ratio of at least five positive interactions for every negative one. This includes affirmations, compliments, and expressions of gratitude. Make it a habit to:
   - Acknowledge your partner's efforts and contributions.
   - Express appreciation for their qualities or actions.
   - Celebrate small victories and milestones together.
2. **Schedule Regular Check-Ins**
   Set aside time each week to discuss your thoughts, feelings, and concerns in a focused and intentional way. Use this time to:
   - Share what's going well in the relationship.
   - Address any challenges or frustrations.
   - Set goals or plans for the upcoming week.
3. **Use a Communication Framework**
   When discussing sensitive topics, follow a structured approach to minimize misunderstandings:
   - **Step 1:** Start with a positive statement or appreciation (e.g., "I love how thoughtful you are.").
   - **Step 2:** Share your concern using "I" statements (e.g., "I feel overwhelmed when plans change suddenly.").
   - **Step 3:** Offer a solution or compromise (e.g., "Could we discuss changes ahead of time to avoid confusion?").
4. **Practice Active Listening Exercises**
   Strengthen your listening skills with intentional exercises:
   - **Mirroring:** Repeat back what your partner has said to ensure clarity.
   - **Role Reversal:** Take turns explaining each other's perspectives to foster empathy.
   - **Silent Listening:** Commit to listening without speaking until your partner has fully expressed their thoughts.

Building a Culture of Appreciation

One of the simplest ways to enhance communication is to infuse it with appreciation. Expressing gratitude and admiration creates a positive atmosphere and encourages open dialogue. Consider these practices:

- Write notes or messages expressing what you love about your partner.
- Share specific compliments during conversations, such as, "I admire how patient you were in that situation."
- End each day by sharing one thing you appreciated about your partner that day.

Conflict as an Opportunity for Growth

Conflict is inevitable in any relationship, but it doesn't have to be destructive. When approached with love and respect, conflict becomes an opportunity to strengthen your bond. To navigate disagreements:

- Stay focused on the issue rather than bringing up unrelated grievances.
- Take breaks if emotions escalate, and revisit the conversation when both partners feel calm.
- Seek solutions collaboratively rather than trying to "win" the argument.

Exercises for Enhancing Communication

1. **The Love Language Exercise**
   Discuss each other's love languages (words of affirmation, quality time, gifts, acts of service, physical touch) and how they influence your communication preferences.
2. **Daily Connection Ritual**
   Spend 10–15 minutes each day engaging in uninterrupted conversation. Use this time to share your thoughts, feelings, or simply talk about your day.
3. **Conflict Resolution Practice**
   Role-play a recent disagreement, focusing on active listening and collaborative problem-solving. Reflect on what worked and what could improve.

Conclusion: Communication as the Heartbeat of Love

Communicating with love and respect is a skill that requires intention, practice, and patience. As you integrate these strategies into your relationship, you'll find that even the most challenging conversations become opportunities for connection and growth. Remember, communication is not just about exchanging words—it's about building understanding, trust, and intimacy.

By committing to communicate with love and respect, you and your partner can create a relationship that is both harmonious and resilient, capable of withstanding life's challenges and flourishing in its joys. Let this chapter serve as a guide and inspiration for fostering meaningful dialogue and deepening your connection.

Chapter 3: Rediscovering Shared Hobbies

Shared hobbies are a powerful way to bring couples closer together, offering opportunities to bond, create memories, and foster a sense of partnership. When you and your partner engage in activities you both enjoy, you reignite the spark of connection, laughter, and camaraderie that may have faded over time. Rediscovering shared hobbies is not just about having fun—it's about building emotional intimacy, strengthening teamwork, and finding new ways to celebrate your relationship.

This chapter will guide you through the importance of shared hobbies, how to identify activities that resonate with both of you, and strategies for integrating them into your relationship to enhance your bond.

The Power of Shared Hobbies in Relationships

Participating in shared hobbies provides a range of emotional and relational benefits, including:

- **Rekindling Connection:** Engaging in activities together fosters togetherness and reminds you of why you enjoy each other's company.
- **Building Teamwork:** Hobbies often require collaboration, encouraging you to work as a team and improve communication.
- **Reducing Stress:** Fun activities allow you to unwind, laugh, and escape the pressures of daily life.
- **Creating Memories:** Shared experiences create lasting memories that strengthen your emotional bond.
- **Encouraging Growth:** Exploring new interests together helps both partners grow individually and as a couple.

Reflecting on Past Hobbies

A great starting point for rediscovering shared hobbies is to reflect on activities you once enjoyed together. Consider the following questions:

1. What hobbies or activities did you enjoy at the beginning of your relationship?
2. Are there any traditions or rituals you used to share, such as weekly movie nights or outdoor adventures?
3. What moments of shared joy stand out in your memories?

Revisiting past hobbies can reignite the feelings of excitement and connection you experienced in earlier stages of your relationship. Dust off those board games, revisit favorite hiking trails, or try cooking a recipe that once brought you closer.

Exploring New Interests Together

Sometimes, relationships stagnate because partners fall into predictable routines. Exploring new hobbies together can infuse your bond with a sense of adventure and discovery. To find new interests:

1. **Make a List of Possibilities:** Write down activities you've always wanted to try, such as painting, yoga, or playing a musical instrument. Compare lists to identify overlaps or try each other's suggestions.
2. **Step Outside Your Comfort Zone:** Be open to activities that might feel unfamiliar or challenging. Shared novelty can lead to meaningful growth.
3. **Attend Workshops or Classes:** Taking a class together, whether for dance, photography, or cooking, is a great way to learn a new skill while deepening your connection.
4. **Explore Your Community:** Check local events, clubs, or groups that offer opportunities to engage in shared interests, like community gardening, sports leagues, or book clubs.

Hobbies That Strengthen Relationships

While any activity can be meaningful if you both enjoy it, some hobbies are particularly effective at fostering connection. Here are examples of hobbies that can bring you closer:

1. **Outdoor Adventures:** Activities like hiking, camping, or kayaking provide opportunities to connect with nature and each other.
2. **Cooking and Baking:** Preparing meals together encourages teamwork and creativity. Plus, you get to enjoy the delicious results!
3. **Fitness and Wellness:** Exercising together, whether at the gym or through yoga, promotes physical and emotional well-being.
4. **Creative Pursuits:** Painting, writing, or crafting allows you to express yourselves and create something meaningful.
5. **Games and Sports:** Playing board games, video games, or sports fosters friendly competition and shared excitement.
6. **Music and Dance:** Learning to play an instrument or taking dance lessons can be a fun and romantic way to bond.
7. **Travel:** Exploring new places together creates unforgettable memories and strengthens your sense of partnership.
8. **Volunteering:** Giving back to your community as a team reinforces shared values and builds a sense of purpose.

Overcoming Challenges to Shared Hobbies

It's not uncommon for couples to face challenges when rediscovering or starting new hobbies. Here's how to address some common obstacles:

1. **Different Interests:** If your preferences don't align, consider alternating between activities each partner enjoys. Over time, you may discover mutual interests.
2. **Time Constraints:** Busy schedules can make it difficult to prioritize hobbies. Set aside specific times each week for shared activities, even if it's just 30 minutes.
3. **Uneven Skill Levels:** If one partner is more experienced in a hobby, approach it with patience and a willingness to learn. Focus on the joy of trying something together rather than perfection.
4. **Budget Concerns:** Many hobbies can be adapted to fit any budget. Look for free or low-cost alternatives, such as community events or online tutorials.

Integrating Hobbies Into Your Relationship

To make shared hobbies a regular part of your relationship, consider the following strategies:

1. **Schedule Hobby Time:** Treat hobby time as a non-negotiable part of your week, similar to a date night.
2. **Create Rituals:** Turn your hobbies into traditions, such as a weekly movie night or monthly day trips.
3. **Set Goals:** Work toward shared goals within your hobbies, like completing a puzzle, mastering a dance routine, or training for a 5K together.
4. **Celebrate Successes:** Acknowledge and celebrate milestones, whether it's finishing a project or learning a new skill.

Strengthening Emotional Connection Through Hobbies

Shared hobbies are not just about the activity itself—they're about the emotional connection they create. Here's how to use hobbies to deepen intimacy:

1. **Be Present:** Focus fully on the activity and your partner, avoiding distractions like phones or work.
2. **Communicate Openly:** Share your thoughts and feelings during the activity, whether it's excitement, frustration, or joy.
3. **Support Each Other:** Encourage your partner's efforts and celebrate their achievements, no matter how small.

Exercises to Rediscover Shared Hobbies

1. **The Hobby Brainstorm:** Sit down with your partner and each write a list of hobbies or activities you'd like to try. Compare lists and choose one or two to start with.
2. **The Memory Jar Activity:** Create a "Memory Jar" filled with slips of paper describing activities you once enjoyed together. Draw one at random each week and revisit the activity.
3. **The Monthly Challenge:** Choose a new hobby to explore together each month. At the end of the month, discuss what you liked or didn't like about it.

Conclusion: Rediscovering Joy and Connection

Shared hobbies offer more than just entertainment—they create opportunities for connection, laughter, and growth. By rediscovering old favorites or exploring new activities, you and your partner can strengthen your bond, build lasting memories, and rekindle the joy of being together.

Remember, the goal isn't to be perfect at the hobby or activity but to enjoy the process and celebrate the time spent together. As you embrace shared hobbies, you'll find that the journey of exploration and connection is just as rewarding as the destination. Let this chapter inspire you to prioritize play, discovery, and togetherness as essential elements of a thriving relationship.

Chapter 4: Spontaneity and Surprises

Routine and predictability can provide comfort and stability in a relationship, but over time, they may also lead to stagnation. Spontaneity and surprises breathe fresh life into your connection, rekindling the excitement and passion that often define the early stages of a partnership. Adding an element of the unexpected doesn't just create moments of joy—it strengthens emotional bonds and deepens intimacy.

This chapter delves into the power of spontaneity and surprises, offering practical ideas, psychological insights, and actionable strategies to reignite the spark in your relationship.

The Importance of Spontaneity in Relationships

Spontaneity is about breaking free from routine to embrace moments of excitement, creativity, and unpredictability. It creates opportunities for:

- **Rekindling Excitement:** Introducing novelty keeps the relationship vibrant and engaging.
- **Strengthening Emotional Intimacy:** Thoughtful surprises show your partner that you're thinking of them, fostering a deeper connection.
- **Encouraging Playfulness:** Spontaneous moments often lead to laughter and joy, essential elements of a thriving relationship.
- **Building Positive Memories:** Unexpected gestures become cherished stories and fond recollections over time.

Why Surprises Matter

Surprises go beyond material gifts—they are expressions of thoughtfulness and care that make your partner feel valued. Research shows that surprise activates the brain's pleasure centers, creating a stronger emotional impact than expected gestures. This emotional boost reinforces the bond between partners and strengthens the foundation of your relationship.

Balancing Routine and Spontaneity

While routines provide structure, injecting spontaneity into your relationship prevents monotony. The key is finding a balance:

- Maintain predictable rituals, such as shared meals or bedtime routines, to create stability.
- Add small, unexpected touches to these rituals, such as writing a love note or preparing your partner's favorite drink without being asked.
- Be open to shifting plans occasionally to accommodate spur-of-the-moment adventures.

Types of Surprises to Strengthen Your Relationship

1. **Acts of Thoughtfulness:**
   Small gestures that show you care can have a big impact. Examples include:
   - Leaving a handwritten note on their pillow.
   - Bringing home their favorite snack "just because."
   - Doing a chore they dislike without being asked.
2. **Planned Surprises:**
   Put effort into organizing a special experience for your partner. Examples include:
   - Planning a surprise date night or weekend getaway.
   - Organizing a virtual movie night if you're in a long-distance relationship.
   - Creating a scavenger hunt around your home or town with clues that lead to a meaningful prize.
3. **Spontaneous Moments:**
   Be open to seizing opportunities for fun or connection in the moment. Examples include:
   - Suggesting an unplanned road trip or picnic.
   - Dancing together in the kitchen to a favorite song.
   - Taking a walk in the rain without worrying about getting wet.
4. **Romantic Surprises:**
   Thoughtful, romantic gestures can reignite passion and deepen intimacy. Examples include:
   - Setting up a candlelit dinner at home.
   - Surprising your partner with a heartfelt love letter or poem.
   - Recreating your first date to reminisce about the early days of your relationship.

5. **Gifting Experiences:**
Material gifts are meaningful, but shared experiences create lasting memories. Examples include:
- Booking tickets to a concert, play, or event your partner loves.
- Enrolling in a class together, such as cooking, dancing, or pottery.
- Surprising them with a day dedicated to their favorite activities.

Strategies for Creating Spontaneous and Surprising Moments

1. **Listen and Take Note:**
Pay attention to your partner's likes, dislikes, and interests. Their offhand comments may reveal what would delight them, such as trying a new restaurant or revisiting a favorite spot.
2. **Plan in Secret:**
The element of surprise requires discretion. Coordinate details quietly, and involve trusted friends or family if necessary to ensure your plans remain hidden.
3. **Stay Flexible:**
Spontaneity requires adaptability. Be willing to adjust plans based on your partner's mood, energy level, or unexpected circumstances.
4. **Start Small:**
If surprises feel intimidating, begin with small gestures, such as surprising them with a favorite treat or an impromptu walk in the park.
5. **Make It Personal:**
Tailor your surprises to your partner's personality and preferences. A surprise that aligns with their unique tastes will be far more meaningful.

The Role of Playfulness in Spontaneity

Spontaneity often thrives in an atmosphere of playfulness. Playfulness fosters connection, reduces stress, and makes your relationship feel lighthearted and fun. Ways to embrace playfulness include:

- Engaging in playful teasing or inside jokes.
- Trying silly or unconventional activities together, like karaoke or a dance-off.
- Taking time to laugh together, even during mundane tasks.

Overcoming Barriers to Spontaneity

1. **Fear of Rejection:**
   If you're hesitant to be spontaneous because you're unsure how your partner will react, start with low-stakes surprises. Over time, you'll build confidence and learn what delights them most.
2. **Time Constraints:**
   Busy schedules can make spontaneity feel daunting. Remember that surprises don't have to be grand gestures—small, thoughtful actions can be just as impactful.
3. **Budget Concerns:**
   You don't need to spend a lot of money to create memorable moments. Focus on gestures that show effort and thoughtfulness rather than extravagance.

Ideas for Incorporating Spontaneity and Surprises Into Daily Life

1. **Morning Surprises:**
   Start the day with a thoughtful gesture, like making breakfast in bed or leaving an encouraging note by the coffee maker.
2. **Midday Moments:**
   Send a playful or loving text message during the workday to brighten their mood.
3. **Evening Adventures:**
   Surprise your partner by suggesting an impromptu date, such as stargazing, a movie night, or trying a new recipe together.
4. **Seasonal Surprises:**
   Embrace the spirit of the season with festive activities, like carving pumpkins in the fall, building a snowman in winter, or having a springtime picnic.

Exercises to Cultivate Spontaneity and Surprises

1. **Surprise Jar:**
   Write down ideas for surprises or spontaneous activities on slips of paper and place them in a jar. Take turns drawing a slip each week and carrying out the idea.
2. **The 24-Hour Rule:**
   Commit to surprising your partner with something thoughtful within the next 24 hours. It can be as simple as picking a wildflower on your walk or preparing their favorite dessert.
3. **Bucket List Challenge:**
   Create a shared bucket list of activities you'd like to try together. Select one item to surprise your partner with in the coming month.

Conclusion: The Magic of the Unexpected

Spontaneity and surprises are like the hidden treasures of a relationship, adding layers of excitement, joy, and connection. They remind your partner that they are loved, valued, and thought of in special ways.

Remember, spontaneity doesn't have to be extravagant—it's about infusing your relationship with moments of delight and creativity. By embracing the unexpected, you'll create a dynamic partnership that continues to grow and evolve, keeping the flame of passion alive for years to come. Let this chapter inspire you to explore new ways of surprising your partner and embracing the thrill of spontaneity as a cornerstone of your love story.

Chapter 5: Building a Stronger Future Together

Every successful relationship is a journey, not just through shared experiences in the present but also in the shared vision for the future. Building a stronger future together requires intention, effort, and alignment in goals, values, and aspirations. It is about creating a roadmap for your relationship that honors where you've been, celebrates where you are, and inspires where you want to go.

In this chapter, we will explore strategies for setting relationship goals, strengthening trust and resilience, and fostering a sense of shared purpose. Whether you're navigating challenges or simply seeking to grow as a couple, this guide will help you build a partnership that thrives well into the future.

Why Building a Future Together Matters

The strength of any relationship lies in its ability to evolve. Building a future together ensures that your relationship remains dynamic, intentional, and resilient. A shared vision:

- **Creates Unity:** Working toward common goals fosters a sense of teamwork and alignment.
- **Provides Stability:** Knowing you're both committed to a future together strengthens the foundation of your relationship.
- **Encourages Growth:** Pursuing new aspirations as a couple promotes personal and relational development.
- **Fosters Resilience:** When challenges arise, a shared vision provides motivation to overcome them together.

Reflecting on Your Shared Values and Vision

Before planning for the future, it's important to reflect on the core values that define your relationship. Shared values act as a compass, guiding your decisions and ensuring that you remain aligned as you grow.

1. **Identify Your Values:**
   Sit down together and discuss what matters most to you as individuals and as a couple. Examples of shared values might include honesty, family, adventure, or financial security.
2. **Define Your Relationship Vision:**
   What do you want your relationship to look like in the next 5, 10, or 20 years? Consider:
   - What kind of life do you want to create together?
   - What milestones would you like to achieve as a couple?
   - How do you want to grow emotionally, spiritually, or financially?
3. **Acknowledge Individual Goals:**
   While a shared vision is essential, it's also important to honor individual aspirations. Discuss how your personal goals can coexist with your relationship goals.

Setting Relationship Goals

Goal-setting isn't just for careers or personal growth—it's a vital part of nurturing a strong and thriving partnership. Relationship goals give you both direction and purpose, helping you stay connected and motivated.

Types of Relationship Goals

1. **Short-Term Goals:**
   These are immediate, actionable goals that strengthen your connection in the present. Examples include:
   - Scheduling weekly date nights.
   - Improving communication by practicing active listening.
   - Trying a new hobby together.

2. **Medium-Term Goals:**
   These focus on milestones you'd like to achieve in the next 1–5 years. Examples include:
   - Saving for a major purchase, such as a home or car.
   - Planning a significant vacation or life event.
   - Supporting each other in career or educational pursuits.

3. **Long-Term Goals:**
   These are aspirational goals that shape your vision for the future. Examples include:
   - Building a retirement plan together.
   - Creating a legacy, such as raising a family or contributing to your community.
   - Designing your dream lifestyle, whether that's traveling, starting a business, or living in a particular place.

Steps for Setting Goals Together

1. **Brainstorm:** Write down your individual and shared goals without judgment or filtering.
2. **Prioritize:** Identify which goals are most important and realistic to pursue.
3. **Create a Plan:** Break each goal into actionable steps and assign responsibilities.
4. **Set Deadlines:** Agree on timelines to keep each other accountable.
5. **Celebrate Milestones:** Acknowledge your progress and reward yourselves for achieving goals.

Strengthening Trust and Resilience

A strong future is built on a foundation of trust and the ability to navigate challenges together. Here's how to cultivate these qualities:

Building Trust

1. **Consistency:** Follow through on promises and commitments.
2. **Transparency:** Be open about your thoughts, feelings, and decisions.
3. **Vulnerability:** Share your fears, hopes, and insecurities with your partner.
4. **Forgiveness:** Let go of past grievances and focus on rebuilding trust when it's broken.

Cultivating Resilience

1. **Embrace Change:** Accept that life and relationships evolve. Approach change with curiosity and flexibility.
2. **Support Each Other:** Be your partner's biggest cheerleader during difficult times.
3. **Problem-Solve as a Team:** When challenges arise, work together to find solutions rather than assigning blame.
4. **Practice Gratitude:** Focus on the positive aspects of your relationship to maintain perspective during tough times.

Fostering a Sense of Shared Purpose

Couples who share a sense of purpose often experience greater satisfaction and fulfillment in their relationships. To foster this:

1. **Create Traditions:** Develop rituals that reflect your values, such as celebrating anniversaries in meaningful ways or volunteering together.
2. **Pursue Meaningful Projects:** Collaborate on projects that bring you joy or align with your values, such as gardening, starting a business, or mentoring others.
3. **Support Each Other's Passions:** Encourage your partner to pursue their interests and find ways to participate or cheer them on.
4. **Give Back Together:** Contributing to a cause you both care about strengthens your bond and reinforces your shared values.

Navigating Potential Obstacles

Building a future together isn't always smooth sailing. Here are common challenges and how to overcome them:

1. **Differing Goals:**
   - Solution: Compromise by finding middle ground or supporting each other's goals in turns.
2. **Unforeseen Circumstances:**
   - Solution: Stay adaptable and focus on problem-solving rather than dwelling on setbacks.
3. **Complacency:**
   - Solution: Regularly revisit your goals and vision to keep your relationship dynamic and engaging.

Exercises to Build a Stronger Future Together

1. **The Vision Board:**
   Create a visual representation of your shared goals and aspirations. Include images, words, and symbols that inspire you both. Display the board where you'll see it often.
2. **Future Letters:**
   Write letters to each other imagining where you'll be in 10 years. Share your letters and discuss how you can work together to bring that vision to life.
3. **Annual Relationship Review:**
   Set aside time each year to reflect on your progress, celebrate your achievements, and update your goals.

Conclusion: A Partnership Built to Last

Building a stronger future together is a continuous process of growth, collaboration, and intentionality. By aligning your values, setting meaningful goals, and fostering trust, you create a partnership that is not only resilient but also deeply fulfilling.

Remember, the journey is just as important as the destination. Celebrate each step forward, support each other through challenges, and never lose sight of the love and commitment that brought you together. Your future is yours to shape, and with intention and effort, it can be brighter than you ever imagined. Let this chapter serve as your guide to building a future filled with love, joy, and shared purpose.

Appendix A: Tools for Relationship-Building Exercises

This appendix serves as a comprehensive guide to tools and resources that couples can use to deepen their connection, enhance communication, and strengthen their relationship. Whether you're looking for practical exercises, digital tools, or creative ideas, the tools listed here will help you implement the strategies outlined in the book and customize them to your unique partnership.

1. Communication Tools

Effective communication is the cornerstone of a strong relationship. These tools help couples improve dialogue, express emotions, and resolve conflicts constructively.

Active Listening Cards

- **What It Is:** A set of cards with prompts and questions designed to facilitate meaningful conversations.
- **How to Use:** Take turns drawing a card and answering the question. Examples include "What is something you wish I understood better about you?" and "How can I support you more?"
- **Benefits:** Encourages open communication and deepens understanding.

Conflict Resolution Framework

- **What It Is:** A step-by-step template for resolving conflicts in a structured and respectful way.
- **How to Use:** Follow these steps during a disagreement:
    1. Identify the issue.
    2. Take turns expressing your perspectives without interruption.
    3. Brainstorm solutions together.
    4. Agree on a course of action.
- **Benefits:** Helps couples stay focused on solutions rather than assigning blame.

Nonviolent Communication (NVC) Workbook

- **What It Is:** A workbook based on the principles of Nonviolent Communication, designed to help couples express needs and emotions without conflict.
- **How to Use:** Practice exercises like reframing "you" statements into "I" statements (e.g., "I feel unimportant when plans change suddenly" instead of "You never tell me anything.").
- **Benefits:** Reduces defensiveness and fosters empathy.

2. Intimacy-Building Tools

Intimacy is about emotional closeness, trust, and connection. These tools help couples nurture and enhance their bond.

The Love Languages Assessment

- **What It Is:** A quiz that helps couples identify their primary love languages (words of affirmation, quality time, receiving gifts, acts of service, physical touch).
- **How to Use:** Take the assessment individually, then discuss how to meet each other's love language needs.
- **Benefits:** Encourages couples to express love in ways that resonate most deeply with their partner.

Couples' Journal

- **What It Is:** A shared journal with prompts for reflection and gratitude.
- **How to Use:** Take turns writing entries about your thoughts, feelings, and appreciation for each other. Example prompts: "What made you feel loved today?" and "What is one thing you're excited about in our future?"
- **Benefits:** Creates a record of shared growth and promotes emotional intimacy.

Date Night Jar

- **What It Is:** A jar filled with ideas for dates, ranging from simple activities to more elaborate adventures.
- **How to Use:** Write down ideas on slips of paper, categorize them by cost or time commitment, and draw one when planning your next date.
- **Benefits:** Keeps date nights fresh and prevents falling into a routine.

3. Goal-Setting and Planning Tools

Shared goals and plans strengthen your sense of partnership and align your vision for the future.

Relationship Goal Tracker

- **What It Is:** A printable or digital tool for setting and tracking relationship goals.
- **How to Use:** Write down short-term, medium-term, and long-term goals, and revisit them monthly to assess progress. Examples: "Take a cooking class together" or "Save $5,000 for a vacation."
- **Benefits:** Keeps both partners accountable and motivated.

Future Vision Board

- **What It Is:** A visual representation of your shared aspirations.
- **How to Use:** Create a collage using magazine clippings, photos, and drawings that represent your dreams for your relationship (e.g., a dream home, travel destinations, or family milestones).
- **Benefits:** Clarifies your shared vision and serves as a daily reminder of your goals.

Weekly Check-In Worksheet

- **What It Is:** A structured worksheet for weekly discussions about your relationship.
- **How to Use:** Answer prompts like:
  1. "What went well this week in our relationship?"
  2. "What challenges did we face?"
  3. "What can we do better next week?"
- **Benefits:** Encourages regular communication and prevents issues from festering.

4. Play and Fun Tools

Playfulness keeps relationships vibrant and joyful. These tools encourage laughter and bonding through lighthearted activities.

Couples Trivia Game

- **What It Is:** A game where partners answer questions about each other to see how well they know one another.
- **How to Use:** Write down questions like "What's my favorite childhood memory?" or "What's my dream vacation?" and take turns answering.
- **Benefits:** Encourages conversation and strengthens emotional intimacy.

Improv Adventure Challenge

- **What It Is:** A list of spontaneous activities to try together, such as "Take a day trip without a plan" or "Try a food you've never eaten before."
- **How to Use:** Choose a random challenge and complete it together.
- **Benefits:** Adds excitement and novelty to your relationship.

The Memory Box

- **What It Is:** A box where you store mementos from your relationship, such as photos, tickets, or notes.
- **How to Use:** Periodically revisit the contents together and reminisce about those moments.
- **Benefits:** Strengthens your connection through shared memories.

5. Technology-Based Tools

In the digital age, technology offers innovative ways to enhance your relationship.

Couples Apps

- **Examples:**
    - **Love Nudge:** Helps you align with each other's love languages.
    - **Between:** A private messaging app for couples with features like shared calendars and photo albums.
    - **Raft:** A shared scheduling app to coordinate dates and events.
- **How to Use:** Download the app that best fits your needs and explore its features together.
- **Benefits:** Simplifies communication and planning.

Shared Streaming Playlists

- **What It Is:** A curated playlist of songs, movies, or shows you both enjoy.
- **How to Use:** Create playlists for different moods, such as "Romantic Evening," "Road Trip," or "Lazy Sunday."
- **Benefits:** Builds shared enjoyment and encourages quality time.

Online Classes

- **What It Is:** Virtual courses in cooking, dancing, art, or fitness.
- **How to Use:** Enroll in a class you're both interested in and complete the lessons together.
- **Benefits:** Promotes teamwork and the joy of learning something new.

6. Reflection and Growth Tools

Self-awareness and mutual understanding are essential for a thriving relationship.

Couples' Reflection Cards

- **What It Is:** A set of cards with prompts to explore your relationship's strengths and areas for improvement.
- **How to Use:** Take turns drawing a card and discussing the topic. Example prompts: "What's one thing I do that makes you feel loved?" or "How can we handle disagreements better?"
- **Benefits:** Encourages deep reflection and open dialogue.

Individual Self-Assessment

- **What It Is:** A worksheet to evaluate your contributions to the relationship.
- **How to Use:** Answer questions like:
    - "What's one way I could better support my partner?"
    - "Am I actively listening during conversations?"
- **Benefits:** Promotes self-awareness and personal growth.

Conclusion: Equipping Your Relationship for Success

The tools in this appendix are designed to help you and your partner strengthen your bond, overcome challenges, and create lasting memories. Incorporate these exercises into your routine to maintain a dynamic and fulfilling partnership. Remember, every small effort contributes to building a stronger, healthier, and more joyful relationship.

Message from the Author:

I hope you enjoyed this book, I love astrology and knew there was not a book such as this out on the shelf. I love metaphysical items as well. Please check out my other books:

-Life of Government Benefits

-My life of Hell

-My life with Hydrocephalus

-Red Sky

-World Domination:Woman's rule

-World Domination:Woman's Rule 2: The War

-Life and Banishment of Apophis: book 1

-The Kidney Friendly Diet

-The Ultimate Hemp Cookbook

-Creating a Dispensary(legally)

-Cleanliness throughout life: the importance of showering from childhood to adulthood.

-Strong Roots: The Risks of Overcoddling children

-Hemp Horoscopes: Cosmic Insights and Earthly Healing

- Celestial Hemp Navigating the Zodiac: Through the Green Cosmos

-Astrological Hemp: Aligning The Stars with Earth's Ancient Herb

-The Astrological Guide to Hemp: Stars, Signs, and Sacred Leaves

-Green Growth: Innovative Marketing Strategies for your Hemp Products and Dispensary

-Cosmic Cannabis

-Astrological Munchies

-Henry The Hemp

-Zodiacal Roots: The Astrological Soul Of Hemp

- **Green Constellations: Intersection of Hemp and Zodiac**

-Hemp in The Houses: An astrological Adventure Through The Cannabis Galaxy

-Galactic Ganja Guide

Heavenly Hemp

Zodiac Leaves

Doctor Who Astrology

Cannastrology

Stellar Satvias and Cosmic Indicas

Celestial Cannabis: A Zodiac Journey

AstroHerbology: The Sky and The Soil: Volume 1

AstroHerbology:Celestial Cannabis:Volume 2

Cosmic Cannabis Cultivation

The Starry Guide to Herbal Harmony: Volume 1

The Starry Guide to Herbal Harmony: Cannabis Universe: Volume 2

Yugioh Astrology: Astrological Guide to Deck, Duels and more

Nightmare Mansion: Echoes of The Abyss

Nightmare Mansion 2: Legacy of Shadows

Nightmare Mansion 3: Shadows of the Forgotten

Nightmare Mansion 4: Echoes of the Damned

The Life and Banishment of Apophis: Book 2

Nightmare Mansion: Halls of Despair

Healing with Herb: Cannabis and Hydrocephalus

Planetary Pot: Aligning with Astrological Herbs: Volume 1

Fast Track to Freedom: 30 Days to Financial Independence Using AI, Assets, and Agile Hustles

Cosmic Hemp Pathways

How to Become Financially Free in 30 Days: 10,000 Paths to Prosperity

Zodiacal Herbage: Astrological Insights: Volume 1

Nightmare Mansion: Whispers in the Walls

The Daleks Invade Atlantis

Henry the hemp and Hydrocephalus

10X The Kidney Friendly Diet
Cannabis Universe: Adult coloring book
Hemp Astrology: The Healing Power of the Stars
Zodiacal Herbage: Astrological Insights: Cannabis Universe: Volume 2
<u>Planetary Pot: Aligning with Astrological Herbs: Cannabis Universes: Volume 2</u>
Doctor Who Meets the Replicators and SG-1: The Ultimate Battle for Survival
Nightmare Mansion: Curse of the Blood Moon
<u>The Celestial Stoner: A Guide to the Zodiac</u>
Cosmic Pleasures: Sex Toy Astrology for Every Sign
Hydrocephalus Astrology: Navigating the Stars and Healing Waters
Lapis and the Mischievous Chocolate Bar

Celestial Positions: Sexual Astrology for Every Sign
Apophis's Shadow Work Journal: **:** A Journey of Self-Discovery and Healing
Kinky Cosmos: Sexual Kink Astrology for Every Sign
Digital Cosmos: The Astrological Digimon Compendium
Stellar Seeds: The Cosmic Guide to Growing with Astrology
Apophis's Daily Gratitude Journal

Cat Astrology: Feline Mysteries of the Cosmos
The Cosmic Kama Sutra: An Astrological Guide to Sexual Positions
Unleash Your Potential: A Guided Journal Powered by AI Insights
Whispers of the Enchanted Grove

Cosmic Pleasures: An Astrological Guide to Sexual Kinks
369, 12 Manifestation Journal

Whisper of the nocturne journal(blank journal for writing or drawing)

The Boogey Book

Locked In Reflection: A Chastity Journey Through Locktober

Generating Wealth Quickly:

How to Generate $100,000 in 24 Hours

Star Magic: Harness the Power of the Universe

The Flatulence Chronicles: A Fart Journal for Self-Discovery

The Doctor and The Death Moth

Seize the Day: A Personal Seizure Tracking Journal

The Ultimate Boogeyman Safari: A Journey into the Boogie World and Beyond

Whispers of Samhain: 1,000 Spells of Love, Luck, and Lunar Magic: Samhain Spell Book

Apophis's guides:

Witch's Spellbook Crafting Guide for Halloween

<u>Frost & Flame: The Enchanted Yule Grimoire of 1000 Winter Spells</u>

<u>The Ultimate Boogey Goo Guide & Spooky Activities for Halloween Fun</u>

Harmony of the Scales: A Libra's Spellcraft for Balance and Beauty

The Enchanted Advent: 36 Days of Christmas Wonders

Nightmare Mansion: The Labyrinth of Screams

Harvest of Enchantment: 1,000 Spells of Gratitude, Love, and Fortune for Thanksgiving

The Boogey Chronicles: A Journal of Nightly Encounters and Shadowy Secrets

The 12 Days of Financial Freedom: A Step-by-Step Christmas Countdown to Transform Your Finances

Sigil of the Eternal Spiral Blank Journal

A Christmas Feast: Timeless Recipes for Every Meal

Holiday Stress-Free Solutions: A Survival Guide to Thriving During the Festive Season

Yu-Gi-Oh! Holiday Gifting Mastery: The Ultimate Guide for Fans and Newcomers Alike

Holiday Harmony: A Hydrocephalus Survival Guide for the Festive Season

Celestial Craft: The Witch's Almanac for 2025 – A Cosmic Guide to Manifestations, Moons, and Mystical Events

Doctor Who: The Toymaker's Winter Wonderland

Tulsa King Unveiled: A Thrilling Guide to Stallone's Mafia Masterpiece

Pendulum Craft: A Complete Guide to Crafting and Using Personalized Divination Tools

Nightmare Mansion: Santa's Eternal Eve

Starlight Noel: A Cosmic Journey through Christmas Mysteries

The Dark Architect: Unlocking the Blueprint of Existence

Surviving the Embrace: The Ultimate Guide to Encounters with The Hugging Molly

The Enchanted Codex: Secrets of the Craft for Witches, Wiccans, and Pagans

Harvest of Gratitude: A Complete Thanksgiving Guide

Yuletide Essentials: A Complete Guide to an Authentic and Magical Christmas

Celestial Smokes: A Cosmic Guide to Cigars and Astrology

Living in Balance: A Comprehensive Survival Guide to Thriving with Diabetes Insipidus

Cosmic Symbiosis: The Venom Zodiac Chronicles

The Cursed Paw of Ambition

Cosmic Symbiosis: The Astrological Venom Journal

Celestial Wonders Unfold: A Stargazer's Guide to the Cosmos (2024-2029)

The Ultimate Black Friday Prepper's Guide: Mastering Shopping Strategies and Savings

Cosmic Sales: The Astrological Guide to Black Friday Shopping

Legends of the Corn Mother and Other Harvest Myths

Whispers of the Harvest: The Corn Mother's Journal

The Evergreen Spellbook

The Doctor Meets the Boogeyman

The White Witch of Rose Hall's SpellBook

The Gingerbread Golem's Shadow: A Study in Sweet Darkness

The Gingerbread Golem Codex: An Academic Exploration of Sweet Myths

The Gingerbread Golem Grimoire: Sweet Magicks and Spells for the Festive Witch

The Curse of the Gingerbread Golem

10-minute Christmas Crafts for kids

<u>Christmas Crisis Solutions: The Ultimate Last-Minute Survival Guide</u>

Gingerbread Golem Recipes: Holiday Treats with a Magical Twist

The Infinite Key: Unlocking Mystical Secrets of the Ages

Enchanted Yule: A Wiccan and Pagan Guide to a Magical and Memorable Season

Dinosaurs of Power: Unlocking Ancient Magick

Astro-Dinos: The Cosmic Guide to Prehistoric Wisdom

Gallifrey's Yule Logs: A Festive Doctor Who Cookbook

The Dino Grimoire: Secrets of Prehistoric Magick

The Gift They Never Knew They Needed

The Gingerbread Golem's Culinary Alchemy: Enchanting Recipes for a Sweetly Dark Feast

A Time Lord Christmas: Holiday Adventures with the Doctor

Krampusproofing Your Home: Defensive Strategies for Yule

Silent Frights: A Collection of Christmas Creepypastas to Chill Your Bones

Santa Raptor's Jolly Carnage: A Dino-Claus Christmas Tale

Prehistoric Palettes: A Dino Wicca Coloring Journey

The Christmas Wishkeeper Chronicles

The Starlight Sleigh: A Holiday Journey
Elf Secrets: The True Magic of the North Pole
Candy Cane Conjurations
Cooking with Kids: Recipes Under 20 Minutes
Doctor Who: The TARDIS Confiscation
The Anxiety First Aid Kit: Quick Tools to Calm Your Mind
Frosty Whispers: A Winter's Tale
The Infinite Key: Unlocking the Secrets to Prosperity, Resilience, and Purpose
The Grasping Void: Why You'll Regret This Purchase
Astrology for Busy Bees: Star Signs Simplified
The Instant Focus Formula: Cut Through the Noise
The Secret Language of Colors: Unlocking the Emotional Codes
Sacred Fossil Chronicles: Blank Journal
The Christmas Cottage Miracle
Feeding Frenzy: Graboid-Inspired Recipes
Manifest in Minutes: The Quick Law of Attraction Guide
The Symbiote Chronicles: Doctor Who's Venomous Journey
Think Tiny, Grow Big: The Minimalist Mindset
The Energy Key: Unlocking Limitless Motivation
New Year, New Magic: Manifesting Your Best Year Yet
Unstoppable You: Mastering Confidence in Minutes
Infinite Energy: The Secret to Never Feeling Drained
Lightning Focus: Mastering the Art of Productivity in a Distracted World
Saturnalia Manifestation Magick: A Guide to Unlocking Abundance During the Solstice
Graboids and Garland: The Ultimate Tremors-Themed Christmas Guide
12 Nights of Holiday Magic
The Power of Pause: 60-Second Mindfulness Practices
The Quick Reset: How to Reclaim Your Life After Burnout
The Shadow Eater: A Tale of Despair and Survival

The Micro-Mastery Method: Transform Your Skills in Just Minutes a Day

Reclaiming Time: How to Live More by Doing Less

Chronovore: The Eternal Nexus

The Mind Reset: Unlocking Your Inner Peace in a Chaotic World

Confidence Code: Building Unshakable Self-Belief

Baby the Vampire Terrier

Baby the Vampire Terrier's Christmas Adventure

Celestial Streams: The Content Creator's Astrology Manual

The Wealth Whisperer: Unlocking Abundance with Everyday Actions

The Energy Equation: Maximize Your Output Without Burning Out

The Happiness Algorithm: Science-Backed Steps to Joyful Living

Stress-Free Success: Achieving Goals Without Anxiety

Mindful Wealth: The New Blueprint for Financial Freedom

The Festive Flavors of New Year: A Culinary Celebration

The Master's Gambit: Keys of Eternal Power

Shadowed Secrets: Groundhog Day Mysteries

Beneath the Burrow: Lessons from the Groundhog

Spring's Whispers: The Groundhog's Prediction

The Limitless Mindset: Unlock Your Untapped Potential

The Focus Funnel: How to Cut Through Chaos and Get Results

Bold Moves: Building Courage to Live on Your Terms

The Daily Shift: Simple Practices for Lasting Transformation

The Quarter-Life Reset: Thriving in Your 20s and 30s

The Art of Shadowplay: Building Your Own Personal Myth

The Eternal Loop: Finding Purpose in Repetition

Burrowing Wisdom: Life Lessons from the Groundhog

Shadow Work: A Groundhog Day Perspective

Love in Bloom: 5-Minute Romantic Gestures

The Shadowspell Codex: Secrets of Forbidden Magick

The Burnout Cure: Finding Balance in a Busy World

The Groundhog Prophecy: Unlocking Seasonal Secrets
Nog Tales: The Spirited History of Eggnog
Six More Weeks: Embracing Seasonal Transitions
The Lumivian Chronicles: Fragments of the Fifth Dimension
Money on Your Mind: A Beginner's Guide to Wealth
The Focus Fix: Breaking Through Distraction
January's Spirit Keepers: Mystical Protectors of the Cold
Creativity Unchained: Unlocking Your Wildest Ideas in 2025
Manifestation Mastery: 365 Days to Rewrite Your Reality
The Groundhog's Mirror: Reflecting on Change
The Weeping Angels' Christmas Curse
Burrowed in Time: A Groundhog Day Journey
Heartbeats: Poems to Share with Your Valentine
Dino Wicca: The Sacred Grimoire of Prehistoric Magick
Courage of the Pride: Finding Your Inner Roar
The Lion's Leap: Bold Moves for Big Results
Healthy Hustle: Achieving Without Overworking
Practical Manifesting: Turning Dreams into Reality in 2025
Jurassic Pharaohs: Unlocking the Magick of Ancient Egypt
and Dino Wicca
The Happiness Equation: Small Changes for Big Joy
The Confidence Compass: Finding Your Inner Strength
Whispers in the Hollow: Tales of the Forgotten Beasts
Echoes from the Hollow: The Return of Forgotten Beasts
The Hollow Ascendant: The Rise of the Forgotten Beasts
The Relationship Reset: Building Better Connections
Mastering the Morning: How to Win the Day Before 8 AM
The Shadow's Dance: Groundhog Day Symbolism
Cupid's Kitchen: Quick Valentine's Day Recipes
Valentine's Day on a Budget: Love Without Breaking the Bank
Astrocraft: Aligning the Stars in the World of Minecraft
Forecasting Life: Groundhog Day Reflections
Bleeding Hearts: Twisted Tales of Valentine's Terror

Herbal Smoke Revolution: The Ultimate Guide to Nature's Cigarette Alternative

Winter's Wrath: The Complete Survival Blueprint for Extreme Freezes.

The Groundhog's Shadow: A Tale of Seasons

Burrowed Insights: Wisdom from the Groundhog

Sensual Strings: The Art of Erotic Bondage

Whispered Flames: Unlocking the Power of Fire Play

Forgotten Shadows: A Guide to Cryptids Lost to Time

Six Weeks of Secrets: Groundhog Day's Hidden Messages

Shadows and Cycles: Groundhog Day Reflections

The Art of Love Letters: Crafting the Perfect Message

Romantic Getaways at Home: Turning Your Space into Paradise

Purrfect Brews: A Cat Lover's Guide to Coffee and Companionship

The Groundhog's Wisdom: Timeless Lessons for Modern Life

The Shadow Oracle: Groundhog Day as a Predictor

Emerging from the Burrow: A Journey of Renewal

The Language of Love: Learning Your Partner's Love Style

Authorpreneur: The Ultimate Blueprint for Writing, Publishing, and Thriving as an Author

Weathering the Seasons: Groundhog Day Perspectives

Valentine's Day Magic: A Guide to Romantic Rituals

The Shadow Chronicles: Stories of Groundhog Day

Love and Laughter: Fun Games for Valentine's Day

AstroRealty: Unlocking the Stars for Property Success

The Groundhog's Path: A Guide to Seasonal Balance

Groundhog Day Diaries: Reflections in the Shadow

The Groundhog's Light: Illuminating the Path Ahead

Valentine's Traditions from Around the World

AI Wealth Revolution: Unlocking the Trillionaire Mindset

If you want solar for your home go here: https://www.harborsolar.live/apophisenterprises/

Get Some Tarot cards: https://www.makeplayingcards.com/sell/apophis-occult-shop

Get some shirts: https://www.bonfire.com/store/apophis-shirt-emporium/

Instagrams:
@apophis_enterprises,
@apophisbookemporium,
@apophisscardshop
Twitter: @apophisenterpr1
Tiktok:@apophisenterprise
Youtube: @sg1fan23477, @FiresideRetreatKingdom
Hive: @sg1fan23477
CheeLee: @SG1fan23477

Podcast: Apophis Chat Zone: https://open.spotify.com/show/5zXbrCLEV2xzCp8ybrfHsk?si=fb4d4fdbdce44dec

Newsletter: https://apophiss-newsletter-27c897.beehiiv.com/

If you want to support me or see posts of other projects that I have come over to: **buymeacoffee.com/mpetchinskg**

I post there daily several times a day

Get your Dinowicca or Christmas themed digital products, especially Santa Raptor songs and other musics. Here: **https://sg1fan23477.gumroad.com**

Apophis Yuletide Digital has not only digital Christmas items, but it will have all things with Dinowicca as well as other Digital products.

www.ingramcontent.com/pod-product-compliance
Ingram Content Group UK Ltd.
Pitfield, Milton Keynes, MK11 3LW, UK
UKHW021016050225
454710UK00012B/678